Tea with Cardamom

Warda Yassin

smith|doorstop

Published 2019 by Smith|Doorstop Books
The Poetry Business
Campo House,
54 Campo Lane,
Sheffield S1 2EG
www.poetrybusiness.co.uk

ISBN 978-1-912196-72-2
Designed & Typeset by Utter
Printed by Biddles

Smith|Doorstop books are a member of Inpress:
www.inpressbooks.co.uk. Distributed by NBN International, Airport
Business Centre, 10 Thornbury Road Plymouth PL 6 7PP.

The Poetry Business gratefully acknowledges the support of
Arts Council England.

Contents

For Abtiyo Mohammed Aboker whom I love and miss with equal measure. May you rest in peace.

Victoria Street

If buildings had feelings, Victoria Street
would need a therapist.

Thugs, imams, families, woman beaters,
and a pub, reside in anarchy,

rubble, stray cats and love.
No *Morning* to each other.

The post man knows to knock once.
Children are ushered from pavements

after Maghrib, billowing garnets brush past
sloganed crop tops. The breeze

brings the Adaan, dubstep and sirens,
the smell of the sauna, the smoke of incense.

Out front, my father breaks his fast,
chews dates, offers a cautious smile

to those with heavy eyes across the way.
These parallel buildings demonstrate

difference, but reflect something
of the same. The street is anything

but royal,
we share a common fate.

Cardamom

I'm trying to pinpoint when your mother's love stopped being
the neighbourhood alarm clock on school days; the cardamom songbird
we no longer hear through the walls. It began with you bunking school
for your brotherhood of wayward sons. How did they teach you

to unthread the ropes of her heart? Your Nikes left imprints
the civil war never did. I try to remember the exact moment
your school teachers felt vindicated. Your extra-terrestrial eyes,
bruised and hard. The only required information.

How did you become a statistic and not the space between zero
and one, where love lies? I think of the moment your mother became
homeless in her Dubai imported living room. Threading the years
into abaayas and daughters, serving tea without cardamom.

Was there a day you tried to teach her war was safe – the charred feet,
burning neighbourhoods, familiar limbs, counting heads? The running
and the loss, the losing, and the praying next to your empty bed?
Why didn't you learn that mothers turn into refugees when we leave?

Abaaya – A modest dress

At 57

Nasra changed the entire decor, ripped up the carpet,
put her bed by the window and his cupboard by the door.
She threw away his bedside dates, dry without his warmth,

and stole away the gabays, prescriptions, his brown leather jacket
from prying eyes. She placed her vanity box by his old radio
to hide the truth; the dim lit hallway looks like him at night.

The coffee table is still swarmed with his books: the Quran,
Sunnah, Dreams of my Father. She envies the spines. Yesterday,
she wore his shoes to garden, her toes somehow finding the soil.

Gabays – Somali poetry
Sunnah – Words by Prophet Muhammed SAW

In Burco

The house had no stairs. It was one floor
and the shower was roofless. Rain fell in like a waterfall.
There were blow-dryers trailing from four sockets.

The streets were covered in sand but always required shoes.
Scholars were young and quick-footed. Vendors pushed
wheelbarrows full of money like vegetables.

My uncle had an in-house Arabic school. In the hallway,
young boys chimed Tajweed in unison. The air was heavy
with unsi smoke and home.

Outside, girls wore jilbabs like amethysts against
the Maghrib sky. Inside, they wore mobile phones,
remedies, well-kept braids and heartbreak.

At night, it was a city of hotels and dreams, where rental
Range Rovers carried young guests to Plaza. I found myself
reflected in every single one.

Buses were open trucks that flew over bumps. The army
was the police, the police drove tanks. My mother
slapped me for staring.

Burco – A city in Somaliland
Tajweed – The correct pronunciation of the Quran for recitation
Unsi – Frankincense
Jilbabs – A type of Somali women's outer garment

Small Talk

You ask for my tribe before my telephone number,
then my city. And even though we both know
it isn't the thing to say, you tell me your grandfather swore
Men of honour can tiri lineage back to the start.

I say *My father taught us we are all citizens of our country,*
and *people of the land. But I am a woman of my own village.*

By the time we walk across Blackfriars Bridge, I want to
advise you on closed-toe sandals, overseas universities. We fall
into speaking Somali. I've never worn a country before,
but you make me wear it like a green dirac catching the light.

Tiri – To count
Dirac – A traditional party dress

Facts & Trivia

On her three day journey, my Grandmother would pass lions
on her way to Abo's boarding school.

On a midmorning, after Malacamad, my Dad's school friend
was attacked by a crocodile.

I'm scared of dogs, even when they don't bark.

On a curfew night, my mother watched her uncles get shot
through the back of the head, by the military.

When the war began, my aunt was detained between borders
like a pattern trapped under tapestry.

I love gold eye shadow and reading books about war.

On his travels in India, my uncle received a letter
documenting the death of his beloved uncle.

My cousin fell in love in Libya, around the time
she no longer had to bind her femininity.

I cry at rom coms and classic tearjerkers.

On a moonless night, my paternal great grandparents
were massacred for being different.

This year, in a land far away, my Abtiyo was lowered
home, and I prayed my first Janazah.

On verandas, by bedside lamps, on living room carpets,
I set down their stories.

Malacamad – Islamic school
Janazah – Funeral prayer

Stories of Boys and Men

I know of boys who have killed and have been killed, boys
who would die for postcodes and houses they do not own, who hold
their 14 year old brother's hand and mould it around knives, hammers
and blades, their knuckles unkissed gang signs.

I know of husbands who sleep lopsided, one eye on the fire
escape, the other on a nursing wife. Wallahi she's seen the back of him
running more times than she's opened the front door to his Salam.
They are tired of hiding the hagbaad and Ayeeyo's gold.

I know of boys who smile at me in respect, whose names
paralyse the ear, boys who I differentiate by dusk and dawn
with their limited light. I know of young men who've survived
desert walks along Godless plains, Kenyan refugee camps

inside crates, the grieving sea, cold hands feverishly pulling at fabric.
Those who died to arrive safe. I know of fathers who burned
their memories and frayed their tongues; men who have gained
nothing, whose children are conscripted to the war they fled,

turning the streets, the living rooms, their mother's wombs
into graveyards. And I know those women who wear emptiness
like phones that ring out unanswered, mothers whose backs buckle
under the weight of storms. I know of sisters who keep tally.

Wallahi – I swear by Allah
Hagbaad – A traditional way to save money
Ayeeyo – Grandmother

Sheffield Children's Hospital

Hand drawn fishes float on indigo walls and Looney Tune
picture books sit on the window sill. You lie there, quartered,
tight-lipped, telling Ayeeyo she knows nothing. I can see
how you pretended to be a man for so long. Abtiyo teases you
about visitors and handmade love notes with smudges,
three girlfriends on the go, English, Arabic, Somali.
You pretended to be 18. The punctures tear at your ribs.

And every few minutes, the weight of your world loosens,
the grip on your phone wanes, and the gates of your eyes close.
Then you jerk awake, eyeball the room, swear people only care
when you're stabbed, in prison or dead. We coax you to drink water
by reminding you it needs you. You're everything but scared.
I leave you nestled between Hooyo's breast and Abo's gallows,
watching rapid-fire cartoons, but seeing nothing.

Abtiyo – Maternal uncle
Abo – Father
Hooyo – Mother

Weston Park

I found the photograph in the brown suitcase with the clipped passports,
grandfather's cassettes and those old red NHS logbooks.

Hooyo is wearing an oversized white T-shirt and her sinewy curls
scamper across her shoulder blades, jet black eyes dare the moon.

Now, she will tell me these were unruly days of impromptu photo shoots,
ankle deep in primroses, the loneliness of motherhood in Edward Street flats.

Aragsan's henna buzz-cut is the focus, turning everything bokeh,
even then ironclad, her smile reminding you why she married last.

One day, she will succumb to the community and gift her daughter with all
the ways to remain kind and good and modest. Then there's Abdisalam

who's only Abdi here. His face framed by a cloud of afro, ebony skin stark
against a sanguine smile. Soon, he will learn to answer to a half-name

as he juggles a half life – weekdays spent scolding sons for eyebrow slits
and fades; those Sundays longing to cut across his boyhood mountains.

His Passport

Her border had once been the length of him. Her horizon
the width of his thinning arms, each meeting now sealed within
a strange checkpoint, each longing a trespass.

But her homeland remained his face, the dabagalle squirrel
his jaw, the wisdom of scholars his ears, the Horn of Africa
the land between his eyes, her touch his eyelashes.

Once, his passport had been a meydi tree, rooted in the frankincense
she has wafted through years of houses, the scent welling inside
the new suitcase, its unworn shirts, expensive fabrics, pocket Quran.

Now she is ceaseless, reciting Ayat- Al Kursi over the phone,
telling him time is relative to the distance between
the Indian Ocean and the English Channel.

In this final hour, there are no documents to allow her to enter
into his arms, to gently ruffle the hospital covers to wake him for Fajr,
to wash his body, read his Janazah prayer.

Dabagalle – Squirrel
Meydi – Type of frankincense tree
Ayat- Al Kursi – a verse from the Quran used for protection
Fajr – Dawn prayer

A Love Like Skies

I'd be a curtain of constellations
in my velvet abaaya. The eclipse,

our blinds closed for privacy.
Heaven: the realm where we come together

like rain to ocean to vapour,
our parting and starting over.

Fajr and Maghrib our greetings.
We'd be the guardians of all birds,

teach them how to fly
by enveloping the wind.

Seamstress

that bans all things natural and pretty, you work underground
sewing thoughts with your hands, tailoring ideas that were torn
from your true discourse. You who fight to endure
the shadows of a city that suppresses simple liberties.

Your dissent in the market place, whispering *believe*
to other shrouded sisters of grief. You share when you should not.
But compassion knows no rational thought, and your heart
is a sanctuary, a safe haven to all breathers.

Seamstress of life, yours are the beads of the river,
the embroidery of the night, in the city that mourns the sun,
you are the new-born, weaving hope,
to be celebrated, to be worn.

My Sisters

have given me an insult-proof vest.
They shot me first, gifting me with armour
against the sting of others' words.
Now I'm immune to the insults of the universe.
Ayan cares for nothing,
Zuhur is unbeaten at scoffing,
Sundus is wide-eyed and watching,
Ikram taught me about plotting,
so my secrets are spoilt with options.
Each has advice, purple, green, red and orange.
My sisters would have been my friends
long before God intervened with blood.
They remind me to release my forked tongue,
to reject calls when they're in the wrong.
They are unruly teachers,
with lessons in how to grow.
They assure my soul
it is the best they know.

Trophy Wife

We still don't know the whole of it,
what made you fall out of favour with your skin,
torch your make up and learn to love

black seed oil. Babygirl, your mother and I
missed you that year, we froze your favourite
pearlescent highlighter, didn't know how its name

Trophy Wife would become you,
how you would wipe the shine from your cheekbones
before entering his Audi, pull the lashes from the eyes

he told you belonged to him. Powerless, we waited
for you to combust. But you did not char. Girl, the day you left
we saw you strut, all amber glow – the coals of you burning.

Blick

I told my sister we should start a revolution
and reclaim this word – blick. Because I'm so blick
like tarmac on a freshly laid road in a close-knit community,
like the dabqaad of charcoal burning the frankincense
smoking under a mother's garments. Blick, blicker than
your coffee on a Monday morning, blick with a Vaseline sheen,
blicker than any sheep, no cling film wrap or bottled bleach.
I'm the sky's landscape; my elbows ashen-topped boulders
silhouetting the night, my cheeks, the sun's promise of staying.

The first man to read the Adaan was Bilal who was blick,
the Noor of his face filtering through the moonlight, the timbre
of a voice heard by all. And he and those of us who are blick
are as coal-strong as a furnace in a northern factory, as dark
as my father's village after rain. Have you ever been held
by the night, her strong, blick arms cloaking you from this
alabaster world? Whenever I am tired, she'll turn off the light,
allow me to disappear into kinder shadows, embroider
my mother's body into the nocturnal sky.

Dabqaad – An incense burner
Noor – Light
Bilal ibn Rabah – The first man to lead the call to prayer

A Mother's Storm

It took a hurricane to bring her closer to the landscape.
And so it came, from the nature of her womb
a whirlwind of pirate ships releasing their leverage,

devastated her from the shore.
It took an earthquake, never before
recorded on the Richter scale,

to move her from bed.
She howled as they paid their respects.
Her piousness stopping her from reminding them –

He is not dead,
just momentarily lost.
And the people of Pompeii must have hid

and Anne Boleyn must have prayed
for a pardon to see fit
that a tsunami is a puddle before it becomes big.

So who is Mother Nature to give up on him?
He is basketball,
not the spoils of war.

His eyelashes the envy of all.
His heart beat with hers once,
and her thunder would will it back.

First line from 'Hurricane Hits England' by Grace Nichols

Learning the Janazah Prayer

It's been a while since we sat in Mother's living room
without Universal TV blaring out over perfumed house guests.

She pulls the fringes of the mat, teaches us the prayer
every parent avoids and Arabic school forgets.

Hooyo, it's swift. You must ensure your intentions are clear,
and make wudu, you remember the routine, yes?

We stand in rows like soldiers there to learn the ways
of the second life. *You can use whatever language you like.*

Hooyo, do not bow, there is only oath and dua between you
and Allah, stay shoulder to shoulder with your sisters.

Later, I practise and learn how you can never be taught
how it feels to breathe for the first time. So I pray

you were cleansed like hail after a storm, housed
in an abode made from light, dark beautiful hands

nursing the daughter you never had, waiting for her
and the best of us to join you, *ameen.*

Wudu – Ritual washing for prayer

Sabr and Iman

that the visitors repeat these words, the men hover by the door,
the women reposition my shalmad, smooth the stray hair

that I'm tired of being told not to cry by men, who know loss
like warmongers, and those who came through duty

that I fell to the ground and bit my tongue till it tore, fearful
of haram grief, and astigfirallah, for a moment I longed to join him

that I returned home, legs collapsed, hijab coiled around my neck,
stunned skin to the bare floor, till I found you cradling me in 1997

that the stove stayed empty and my neighbours forgave my manners,
Edo Safiyah's unwashed dishes, little bowls of cold popcorn

last night, I lay in your old room remembering your moonlight forehead,
journeyed to where I planted a small cherry tree above you

your night-shaded palms; a gift to open-mouthed birds. Oh Allah,
how I wish I could have pocketed an inch of his Sabr and Iman.

Sabr means patience and Iman means faith. The saying can often be used as a comfort for
those who are grieving.
Shalmad – A long shawl draped over the shoulder
Astigfirallah – God forgive me

Tales

I want to read a novel about Somalis that isn't trauma porn.
Set it before the war and after my grandfather's birth. In this story,
we're wearing 70s olive oil afros, décolletage bare on family photos,
backdropped by hand-painted palm trees and ocean views.

We're not pirates, but mermaids lazing by crystalline lagoons, shiid
hoisted to the waist, buoyant youths swimming to jaamacad in coral crowds,
the rainforests of our sea. On the beach there is no blood, only vendors
reciting poetry, and there are no droughts on these dry pages, turn a leaf

and drift to the souq at dhur and see how we barter and flirt
in the baking hours, wearing the richness of our language in idle talk
like well-oiled summers. In the spine of this book, school girls will fall
in illicit love on abandoned Ferris wheels, then emerge mighty

from girlhood like the mountains of Sheikh. Our men will be the heroes,
for once, their webbed hands scaled in tenderness. The word colonialism
is nowhere in this manuscript, and the epilogue speaks of a character afloat
with handed-down culture, waving off Ayeeyo returning to Berbera.

The antagonists will be us swimming in deep water, for we cannot exist
without fault. And we do not need to look to other lands for treasures to adorn
it – abundant geels, coal, frankincense, hand-drawn depictions
of nomads, and shining green-blue diracs billowing from its title.

Jaamacad – University
Geel – Camel

24

Searching for My Father's Tree

I expected a willow tree with an answer as to why
my father never wears jeans. Its sturdy bark able to withstand
a field of fallen kin in the *Year of Malaria*.

We translated it as *rip at the back* and he allowed us to.
With each leaf, I imagined a testimony to the years
spent in post-colonial schools, never learning

to hate his face. My father's tree, the only tree
in this abaar, holding onto something, its small cuts
like sun-dried lips speaking his name. When I found it,

a spectacle at dawn, a wayfarer rooted, where Ayeeyo
birthed him into the palms of our village –
oh Father, the flowering hibiscus growing at its base.

Abaar – Drought

Acknowledgements

First and foremost, all thanks to Allah for blessing me with this opportunity. This pamphlet would not have been possible without the support, inspiration and love of my family and friends. May Allah shower you with his blessings. You have allowed me to write about what I need to and given me endless inspiration along the way. Thanks for the stories, memories and moments, of which there are too many to count. I give special thanks to my Hooyo and Ayeeyos for being the warmest warriors I know, and to my community for being a great space to grow and learn. Thanks to my dearest father, brothers, sisters, cousins, aunts, uncles and family I love you with all my heart.

I also thank Vicky Morris, who has championed me throughout my writing journey, taught me much and inspired me to continue to grow as a writer. You selflessly help so many creative young minds and I value you greatly as a mentor and a friend.

To the Hive South Yorkshire young writers network, Vicky Morris, Nik Perring and all my fellow emerging young writers who create such a safe space at Hive's Saturday group – thank you! I appreciate your feedback and communal support. You guys are amazing writers and, most importantly, people.

Thank you also for the other guidance and opportunities I've had along the way including from the Writing Squad and Steve Dearden, The Poetry Business, Verse Matters, Off the Shelf Festival and Arvon. Thanks to writers such as Helen Mort, Peter Sansom, Hannah Lowe and all those who have inspired me in workshops and readings along the way. Thanks also to Eleanor Holmshaw and Suzannah Evans at the Poetry Business.

Thank you to the editors of the following anthologies: *Verse Matters* (Rachel Bower and Helen Mort), *Halfway Smile* and *Everyday Hymn* (Vicky Morris), *Introduction X* and *The North* (Smith|Doorstop), for publishing versions of these poems.

Many thanks to Kayo for believing in my work, and to The Poetry Business for supporting young people in the North with great workshops and opportunities and making this all possible and for your patience and warmth.